PHEASANT PLUCKER

LILY BEVAN

‖ SAMUEL FRENCH ‖

samuelfrench.co.uk

FOR AMATEUR PRODUCTION ENQUIRIES

UNITED KINGDOM AND WORLD EXCLUDING NORTH AMERICA
plays@SamuelFrench-London.co.uk
020 7255 4302/01

Each title is subject to availability from Samuel French, depending upon country of performance.

RADAR

ABOUT THE AUTHOR

LILY BEVAN

Lily trained at RADA and studied Social and Political Sciences at Jesus College, Cambridge. Acting credits include: *A Voyage Round My Father* (Donmar Warehouse); *Kindertransport* (Shared Experience, Hampstead Theatre and National Tour); *The Miser* and *The Hypochondriac* (Belgrade Theatre, Coventry); *Dr Who* (BBC) and *Rumpole of The Bailey* (BBC Radio).

Writing credits include: *Talking to Strangers* (co-written with Sally Phillips, BBC Radio 4), *Mock Tudor* (Pleasance Edinburgh, Theatre 503), *The People of the Town* (RADA), *A Stab in The Dark* (Calder Theatre, Latitude Festival), *Avocado* (co-written with Bekah Bunstetter, Kings Head Theatre, Playwrights Horizons NYC), *Café Red* (Old Red Lion Theatre, Trafalgar Studios) and *Stephen & The Sexy Partridge* (co-written with Finnain O'Neil) Old Red Lion Theatre/Trafalgar Studios.

Directing credits include: *The Death of All Elephant Elders* by Bekah Bunstetter, Finborough Theatre – nominated Best Director, Off-West End Awards. Lily was a semi-finalist for the Funny Women Awards 2015.

Lily attended the Royal Court Young Writers Programme and the Emerging Writers Group at the Bush Theatre, studied screenwriting at NYU and performing with Philppe Gaulier in Paris.

Lily is a trained yoga teacher with a liking for extended metaphors, has a BAGA 4 in gym, and blogs for The Huffington Post UK and USA.

FOREWORD BY EMMA THOMPSON

Lily Bevan is one of the finest, funniest and most original writers I know.

I have been reading, watching and sometimes even performing her work for a few years now and it gets better and better.

I feel a strong kinship with it and with her because of writing and performing my own material for television and for the Edinburgh Festival quite a long time ago. There are so many memories. Bear-baiting, warm gin, mud wrestling but principally, naked fear. The show I wrote was a review – comic monologues, songs and the like and it featured some very odd extras. I played a gorilla at one point. Lily plays a falcon. You can feel the audience re-organising its mind around the unfamiliar. It's edgy work but exciting when it comes off.

Women's comedy is different to the male archetypes. It follows different rules and rhythms. I am not sure how much has changed in the comedy world since I was a girl, if I'm honest. I know it is still a struggle to find your place in amongst all the male voices and I also know it requires courage to shoulder your way in and be different – *Pheasant Plucker* comes from one of those brave new talents. It's hilarious and wonderfully surprising.

Enjoy.

Emma Thompson
New York, April 2016

Pheasant Plucker premiered at Underbelly in August 2015 as part of the Edinburgh Fringe Festival.

It then played at The Bush Theatre, London, in November 2015 as part of RADAR Festival.

Pheasant Plucker Creative Team

Written & Performed by
Lily Bevan

Director
Hannah Eidinow

Assistant Director
Lois Jeary

Assistant Producer
Emma Pritchard

Stage Manager
Sarah Tryfan

Stage Manager, Underbelly Weeks 3 & 4
Tom Clutterbuck

Designer
Simon Wells

Marketing
Suzanna Rosenthal

PR
Gaby Jerrard PR

Musician/Narrator
Luke Courtier

Movement Director
Polly Bennett

Illustrator
Eleanor Brough

To Peter, Jane, Sophie, Lorna and Sarah.
And to Emma, for the Edinburgh pint just at the right moment.

Featuring monologues from the BBC Radio Four series *Talking to Strangers* produced by BBC Studios.

AUTHOR'S NOTE

My first series of monologues was called *Avocado* co-written with New York playwright Bekah Brunstetter for the Kings Head Theatre in 2009. Since then I've enjoyed writing monologues as a special glimpse inside a character's thoughts.

Pheasant Plucker introduces us to Harriet, an inquisitive falconer, whose time has come to go and see the world.

Ever since playing a Rentokil exterminator for my final RADA showcase I've been on the lookout for new writing for women with a bit of urgency and daftness.

Pheasant Plucker required a lot of previewing in London before it flapped up to Edinburgh, and the creative team were integral to its support and development. One of my favourite things is collaboration and connection, the best thing about working alone was in fact getting to work with a team of brilliant people.

Very many thanks to them: Sarah Tryfan, Hannah Eidinow, Lois Jeary, Eleanor Brough, Luke Courtier, Simon Wells and Tom Clutterbuck, Polly Bennett and Emma Pritchard. As well as the people who read and listened and gave great feedback including Lorna Beckett, Jeany Spark, Jim Rastall and Will Rastall.

I have enjoyed this. I have never fully understood it. Let me know if you do.

FURTHER THANKS TO

Jess Search, Beadie Finzi, Isabel Shapiro, BRITDOC, Laura Rourke, Maggie Service, The Black Swan, Sally Phillips, Sam Bryant, Polly Bennett, Jessica Swale, Blanche McIntyre, Polly Findlay, Gaby Jerrard, Suzanna Rosenthal PR and team, The Museum of Comedy, Chris Thompson, Michael Sheen, Madani Younis, Rob Drummer, Lizanne Crowther, Bush Theatre Team, RADA, The Leicester Square Theatre, Marina, Vikki and Fi at Underbelly, Underbelly Daisy Team, Lorna O'Leary, Jim Keegan, Nicholas Barter, Geoff Bullen, Bekah Brunstetter, Monobox, Emma Anacootee-Parmar, Sarah Wolf, Bryony Fraser, Rosie Sheehy, Alice Robinson, Miztli Neville, Gaia Wise and Pat Myers.

Poster/Book Cover Photography by Lily Bevan shot by Bronwen Sharp

Design by Matthew Smith at Desk Tidy Design

TIPS FOR PERFORMANCE

The *Pheasant Plucker* script could be used in different ways. There are nine characters within. It could be done in its entirety as a one-woman show, running at about fifty-five minutes, with one performer playing all parts. It could be used to pick out separate monologues. It could be done by a cast, with one actor playing each character.

Accents: accents are suggested in the character list. I use them, often highly fallibly, to knock me out of my own vocal rhythms and jig myself about a bit. Use them, change them or ditch them.

Staging: *Pheasant Plucker* was originally performed with a projector and a series of about a hundred slides. These images acted as a backdrop, suggesting location, ambience, cock balloons etc. Projectors are common in Edinburgh shows due to quick turnaround, but there are lots of other ways to stage the show. I organised my costumes and props in and around a silver birch tree to impart a hint of Harriet's field in the countryside. Mainly because I like silver birch trees.

Costumes: I used small bits and pieces of costume for different characters, Harriet wore yellow wellies (making her distinct), Irenie wore a tweed blazer, Jester wore a feathered gilet, a cardboard beak and smoked a fag. But you can do anything you fancy, or none at all.

Narrator: for Edinburgh I performed the show alone. For the Bush I had a narrator who was a musician, my mate Luke, who sang links between the scenes. You can cut these lines or keep them, record them to be played as sound cues, or cast an actor or musician.

Where possible I have put avian references in the music/text/set/costumes - a bird chorus. A song often used through my show was *King* by Years & Years which had come out that Summer. We played it in pre show, Harriet sings it, Narrator sings it and the final dance duet was danced to it. Do use it too, or avian themed songs might work too, like *Wind Beneath My Wings*.

CHARACTER LIST

HARRIET – From Norwich, a falconer, wears yellow waterproofs and wellies and a falconer's gauntlet.

YOGA TEACHER – Soothing gentle voice, has been told that using metaphors is the best way to teach yoga.

THERAPIST – In the text the therapist is unseen, but could be played by an actor where some lines could be added.

PALM READER – Australian, rambunctious, likes to work the "hen do" circuit.

REMI TICTOC – French, an expensive nutritionist.

DANIEL SACHET – A debonair actor of a certain age.

TUDOR PHEASANT PLUCKER – Harriet's grandmother – very game.

IRENIE – Extremely posh, quite hard to understand at times, jolly, jolly.

JESTER – Cockney, a falcon, smoking a fag, very laissez-faire.

NARRATOR/ MUSICIAN – Optional (see tips for performance).

Pre show. A projector with slides (please see back of book for slide list).

Slide: "Pheasant Plucker" by Lily Bevan

> *A field.*

> *A silver birch tree. A few props and costumes hang on its branches. Grass. Leaves.*

> *A* **MUSICIAN** *sits on a grassy knoll and sometimes sings narration.*

> *Pre-show music recorded or by* **MUSICIAN**

> *Music: soaring anthemic American prairie type music.*

> **HARRIET** *enters the field wearing wellies, waterproofs, a falconer's gauntlet, and shiny 80s sunglasses. She acknowledges the crowd of spectators, then glances at the sky. (Slide 1)*

HARRIET Yip. Yip.

Ladies & Gents. Eyes to the skies.

Jester should have been back by now. But I can't see him. Which is unusual. Yip Yip.

Now what I'm going to do is lure him back with a nice piece of steak. (**HARRIET** *takes a steak out of her bag*) I'm going to circle the steak around my head, throw it up into the air, and Jester will swoop down and catch it in his beak, but keep your eyes peeled as my falcon is fast. (*Throws the steak up, it flops down, she looks* *up, no)* Unusual. Jester is a peregrin falcon. Latin name – Falco peregrinus.

Sometimes he just doesn't want steak. I've got a rat on a string. I'm going to chuck the rat up.

HARRIET *takes a small rat tied to a string out of her bag and circles it around her head*

Yip Yip.

Falco peregrinus. Known in the USA as the duck hawk. But he is not a duck. And he is not a hawk. He is a falcon. And his fastest speed is 242 miles per hour. Faster than a Lamborghini. Slower than a ringwraith. At a guess. Only one country you will not find him in. (*To audience*) Can you guess? New Zealand.

Yip Yip. Unusual.

Harriet and Jester, we're a team. He's called Jester because he likes to play tricks and be naughty. I tell him little jokes: "Hey Jester, when should you buy a bird? When it's going cheap." I sing him little songs (*sings, badly and loudly*). I'm wearing these sunglasses so that he doesn't peck out my eyes. I've got this little hood so I can blindfold him so if he tries to peck out my eyes he can't see where they are.

Yip Yip.

He might be confused by the sun, or he's lost track of time, or he's using his height, the higher he goes, the faster he can fly back in, he might be trying to kill me?

Excellent eyesight... he could see and kill me even at night, in snow.

(*loud call*) HO. No.

We have peregrin falcons nesting in Norwich Cathedral and a favourite spot is the roof of Anne Summers on Diss High Street.

Let's all bring him in now. Give me a ho... Everyone 123 Ho!

I mean falconry is a weird life. In a way. I could sort of do without this. I'm here in this field 24/7 – last week I ate one of his frozen rats thinking it was a Calippo, I never go on dates, I only wear yellow... it's just Jester Jester – you know – hey ho no he's fucked off. Maybe I'm glad, maybe I'm glad he's fucked off... maybe I should fuck off and do the things normal people do... become a people person and not a bird person.

I'm from this family of bird handlers dating all the way back to medieval pheasant pluckers...it's just birds, birds, fucking birds...everywhere I go I see birds...hey ho yip no. (Stop)

Fine Jester. You're not the only one who can spread their wings, go on an adventure. I'm throwing down the gauntlet.

HARRIET *throws down the gauntlet. (Slide 2)*

I could be as free as a falcon, as agile as the sharp-shinned hawk, as vocal as the cedar waxwing, as sociable as the yellow-rumped warbler, as bold and perky as the tufted titmouse.

Where the shit is he?

It's ok for birds. No bus stops. No Brexit. No smear tests. Owls can do that thing where they turn their head all the way round. Wouldn't I like to do that? Yes, actually. Do I like being a bi-ped on £11 an hour, not I do not. But this is what I do and this is how he treats me.

You feathery bastard! Fickle friend! Traitor! You've shown me up in front of these people. God, he's probably hanging out by the pussy willows laughing his tits off.

HARRIET *makes a list in a diary of her plans.*

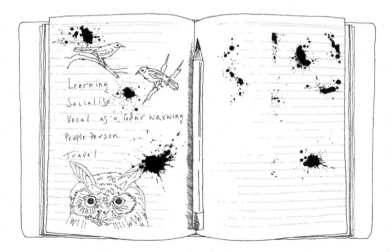

I'm going to fly the nest to pastures new...become a people person, not a bird person. I'm going to go to London, where people are all sane and sorted out, right? I'm going to read *Time Out* and do Groupons and find some classes, and go to yoga, get healthy and meet experts. See what's out there – yip yip *(swearing – V sign)* Jester...yes, thank you Jester.

First stop. Yoga class...

Train sound as **HARRIET** *crosses stage.*

MUSICIAN

Sings.
YOGA CLASS,
"PEOPLE PEOPLE" DO YOGA CLASS,
IT SLOWS YOU DOWN WHEN YOU'RE GOING FAST,
GET A REALLY NICE SHAPED ARSE,
SIGNING UP FOR YOGA CLASS.

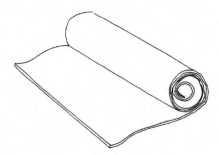

HARRIET *is in the yoga studio. Class is beginning. (Slide 3)*

Music: yoga chanting.

YOGA TEACHER Namaste. Welcome to yoga class. I see we have some new yogis here tonight. Harriet, welcome. So let's begin with a deep collective breath, inhale through the nose and exhale on a HA – HAAA. Inhale and exhale on a HM like the shop HMMM. Peace is your birthright. Peace is your birthright. Peace is your birthright. *(Approaching an audience member, taking their hands, gazing into their eyes)* These are your hands. Let's begin in child's pose. This is a pose...that's like a...tiny adult.

Forehead to the floor and being very careful to *mumble mumble* (**YOGA TEACHER** *'s face on the floor, so becoming unintelligible)* if you don't do that – you are likely to end up *paralysed.*

Arms resting by the sides...like...like a fork and knife either side of a plate. Beautiful.

And breathe. Each breath entering the lungs deeper. Deeper. Inside. Like...a vole, a vole into a hole. That's right. Just listening to the sound of my voice. Like Simon says but without Simon. Just you and the mat. Not Matt – like a guy called Matt. The mat. Not Matt or Simon or anyone. Just you. Following a simple set of movements, of ideas, like a set of chess you've inherited. Or a set of badgers, all the same, all different. But badgers.

Which are movements.

So, slowly coming up onto all fours, into a basic table shape. The back is flat. Flat like a table. Or a bobsleigh. Or a shed

roof. Some shed roofs – some are not. Keep it simple.
Think of the back strong and straight like a… Scandinavian
sofa, like a block of cheese, like a hardback copy of *Wolf Hall.*
Moving through a couple of cat/cow stretches – moo, hiss – but
don't make the noises, it's weird.

Keep breathing.

Raising the hips high like Jesus, spreading the fingers wide,
pressing them into the mat like olives and coming into
downward facing dog like a cat. Release the neck. Release the
neck. Release the neck like a prisoner being released from
prison. Maybe after a couple of appeals. But still served sixteen
years. How the world will have changed. Smart phones. What
are they? Flat whites. Tiny little coffees. Things have seriously
changed…says the prisoner…the neck.

Let it flow.

And raising the right leg toward the ceiling. Imagining there is
no ceiling, just sky and space. And Jupiter and Saturn. Space.
Foot reaching up up, and yes, aliens! With eyes for skin, and
tails at the front, and wisdom. Foot up, up there. And down.
And the left – just keep it in the room.

Feel the difference.

Lowering full body down to a plank. Plank like a plank of wood,
like metal. Engaging the core. Thinking of cores, and of pips,
and of stones, like an avocado. Thinking about how it's hard
to peel an avocado, isn't it? And it's hard to choose a ripe one.
And it's sad when you think you have a ripe one and you get it
home and the bastard is rock hard. Or stringy. And you think
"Fuck me – I paid one pound sixty-five for that!". Plank.

Breathe.

Putting the palm of your foot by the palm of your hand or something. Coming into pigeon like a pigeon. We're going to hold here for four breaths – or nine or five.

Shining the heart forward. Sending your light and energy to... Whales. The big fish, not the small country. But, also, yes, the tiny Celtic country. And...sending the warmth of the heart to the polar ice caps. No don't. They're melting.

MUSICIAN

Sings.
PIGEONS
HMMM.
CAN'T EVEN TOUCH THE TOES
OH BUGGER OFF PIGEON POSE.
WHAT DO LONDON PEOPLE DO?
WHEN THEY WANT TO SELF IMPROVE?
THERAPY.
IF YOUR HEAD IS ON THE BLINK,
BOOK RIGHT IN TO SEE A SHRINK.
THERAPY.

HARRIET *sits in a therapist's office. (Slide 4)*

THERAPIST'S VOICE   "Come in Harriet. You sit over there. Let's begin with a bit about your background."

HARRIET *rummages in a box of stuffed animal toys, choosing, and pulls out a toy farmyard animal. These toys are a collection of anthropomorphic animals, dressed in human clothes, which the therapist encourages clients to use to reenact real life scenarios from their lives.*

HARRIET   *(to* **THERAPIST***)* This one's my mother.

(Slide 5: a toy farmyard animal woman)

This was our house.

(Slide 6: a toy house)

My mother… has three brothers.

(Slide 7: three toy farmyard animals)

This is my father.

(Slide 8: male toy farmyard animal)

He has all kinds of friends.

(Slide 9: many toy animals)

Friends from other countries.

(Slide 10: exotic animals e.g. toy kangaroo and koala)

We used to travel.

(Slide 11: a toy holiday camper)

This is me.

(Slide 12: a toy owl)

This is one of my mates.

(Slide 13: a toy frog)

(Slide 14: back to toy owl. Owl wears a little orange gilet and no pants)

Is it weird that I'm an owl but my parents are goats?

And my friend is a really weird-looking frog?

Is it ok to feel a bit embarrassed?

And like, kind of disloyal?

It's good I can be an owl as I am a bird person, I am quite small and I do wear a gilet. Though I wear pants.

There's no real reason that I chose my mother to be a goat. She should be a bird really. But. You don't have that many.

Well, maybe it was about the pastel clothes...

(Slide 15: toy farmyard animal family)

In the eighties my mother wore a lot of eighties colours – so the goat's clothes are right. My father didn't wear blue postman overalls. But he did wear blue jumpers, so the blue overalls are evocative.

Do you mind me saying I am not sure about this?

I've spent one hundred and thirty-five pounds worth of therapy time re-enacting my problems with animals, and I'm feeling more worried and ashamed about doing this – than anything else that's ever been wrong.

I just thought it would be fun to do some therapy. It's not supposed to be fun, is it? I feel a bit sad about why Jester left but now messing around with the owls and the goats is making me feel a bit sad and completely mad.

Hey, how do you tell the difference between a weasel and a stoat? A weasel is weasily recognised. A stoat is stoatally different.

To the audience.

She's not laughing.

She's gesturing at the box. The characters reminded me of the Sylvanian Families toys I played with as a child, which were manufactured in Japan – but set in an imaginary 1970s middle-class English village. First there were rabbits, foxes, and mice, then they were joined by penguins, elephants, kangaroos. They all live together and enhance each others' lives. They could teach us a lot about harmonious immigration. Mr Farage needs to go to Japan and work for Sylvanian Families. Or maybe Mr Farage just needs to go to Japan so he isn't here.

The Sylvanians have middle-class, successful family businesses, white-collar jobs, large, multi-storey plastic holiday homes, and they go sailing, camping and horse riding. Horse riding is weird when you think about the scale of it.

I am not from the horse-riding class at all. My heritage is the bird-handling class originally. Bumpkins. Crones and pheasant pluckers.

I don't want to live in a Sylvanian Families utopia, but what will my future be? I want to visit a mystic. A palm reader!

A soothsayer – as wise as an owl, deep and full of gravitas…

MUSICIAN

Sings.

MESSING AROUND WITH TOYS,
IT'S ALL JUST A LOT OF NOISE.
ENOUGH OF THE PAST.
LOOK TO THE FUTURE.
CRYSTAL BALLS.

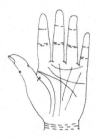

HARRIET *is in the palm reader's salon. (Slide 16: penis balloons)*
A hen party have arrived.

Music: Girls Just Want to Have Fun by Cyndi Lauper.

PALM READER *(Australian)*

Cock balloons, cock balloons, cock balloons!

Hi! Woo hoo! Welcome to the palm reading!

Hello dear, you're a dirty little country bumpkin aren't you –

And we have a hen party in today!

And let's start with you – Helen! Lovely Helen. Did you know
Helen means "Unhealthy Buffalo" in the Navajo Spirit World?
I'm going to look at the palm and tell you how old you are.
Twenty-nine. **(HELEN** *responds)* Twenty-two? Yes. Yes, Looking at
the palm there – I was getting a two and a nine or another two.
Spot on.

Nearly the wedding day. Ding dong. Lovely girls. This is a nice
hen party isn't it? Penis straws. Naughty stories, you've drawn a
little cock on your face there – oh no – it's just your nose and
a portal into the other world. So, that's me. Palm reader and
mystic extraordinaire from the lower hemisphere.

And your role on the day Helen, is? …Bridesmaid is it. Lovely.
(Reads palm) Now looking at the palm – back in the past here,
on the health line – I can see a really good injury aged about
thirteen there. That was falling down a hole. Ssh. Don't speak.
Trampoline? Or a swimming, drowning accident…or just
feeling very hurt, some hurt feelings, or you got very hungry

or…but yes a big event at thirteen. Moving along. Fourteen, fifteen. This line curling up here across the heart line means you were a spoilt child, Helen. This little break in the line here – could be basic unpopularity. You were disliked. She was disliked. But whether you knew it or not remains a great mystery of the spirit world.

Ooh I like weddings.

It won't be a long life, Helen. But it'll be full. Of events. Now the fat side bit here on the hand is something like a lower spine problem. Is that it? Or a blocked colon? Some colon issues. Some Crohn's disease or just a lot of backed up shit, a great deal of stool or diarrhea.

So, that's enough for you. Lovely Helen.

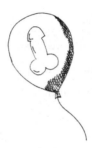

Who's next? What a lovely bunch of girls.

Shona is it? Yes. A cousin. So nice. Groom's side. Aren't you a pretty one. Give me your hand – but not just any hand. Give me your dominant hand. You've picked the left? No, it can't be the left. You need to pick the right. I'm having trouble making out the lines. Which could be because you're really good at clearing things, and effective, or it's dark in here. Or excessive exfoliant use? Or have you been in a fire and burnt off the lines of your hand?

Male spirits will sit to the right of your heart line here, female will sit to your left – someone's hanging around here by this thumb…and he's not very nice.

I'm a bit scared, Shona. So moving on. You. Over there. Pamela? So. The shape of the fingers tells you about your talents…

The thumb – if it's short you are good at numbers, long – good at travel. Yours is average length so stay away from selling holidays.

Second finger – boss finger, so if this is very long – it means you want to take over from the boss, physically you can give him a good old poke in the eye and on a psychic level you're a bit of a bossy boots. I saw Bill Gates's hand, his second finger was about fourteen-foot long. Scientifically proved – this. It's caused by testosterone. Yours is long Pam, you're a boss type – probably with a lot of body hair, bum hair, back hair, probably thick and dark in colour.

Mary – you have a long middle finger – we call this the social worker's finger, not businessy, bit hopeless and tired and kind, shit with money. You are terrible at making decisions. I wouldn't share baths with people.

So here's a general fingering tip girls, I'm not being dirty, Shona don't laugh at that – square fingers are athletic, round artistic, long philosophical, but yours Mary are pointy, diplomatic, you like the fine things – a bit of a collector. Bit of a hoarder. Are you a hoarder there, Mary? Seems so. Got a hundred copies of "Tiny Tits Magazines" or whatever it is you read? A few more puzzles around than are needed at Mary's house.

Now if your fingers are like spatulas – spatularesque, it means – you are intense; dramatic, actors and actresses have those. Big spatula fingers. You should see Jenifer Aniston – big cake lifting digits on her.

Now at last – to the bride – the glowing bride. If your fingers are close together like that – like webbing it's like they need each other, and it means you are very needy – aren't you darl?

Up the side of the hand, these are your attachment lines. You have a lot of lines close together – which means you've been with a lot of men. Let's say – she can't put all her "feelings eggs" in one basket and can't always keep her legs crossed.

Getting married in white? How interesting. Of course white doesn't mean anything these days.

Oh. Look at that. Shame. How does the number forty-nine sound?

I'd get on and swim with the dolphins before forty-nine comes along.

And. Children. It's a bit blank. With a palm like that. Could be no patter. No tiny feet. But then again it might be something about pets.

I'll leave you with that ladies...and I'll see you at the wedding. Except for you Mary, love. Coz I don't think you'll be there.

MUSICIAN

Sings.
HELEN'S ALL BACKED UP WITH SHIT,
DON'T REALLY LIKE THE SOUND OF IT.
NEED TO GIVE THE PIPES A CLEAN,
ONLY EATING BROWN AND GREEN,
START A REGIME.

HARRIET I don't want to die young. So I'm taking myself to see a nutritionist in a (*mispronounced*) vegan café, and she's like...

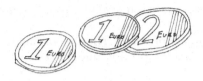

HARRIET *is in the vegan café. (Slide 17)*

Music: French rap/ La belle et le bad boy by MC Solaar.

REMI TICTOC *(French)*

REMI Yeah. Ok. Yeah. Ok. Yeah. Ok. Cool. Yeah.

HARRIET Only it was weird as these sounded like answers but I hadn't asked any questions.

REMI Ok. I am only going to say one thing to you.

HARRIET I was glad she was going to say one thing. I didn't think she was going to say anything at all.

REMI Ok. I am only going to say one thing to you. You need to be clean. You need to be really clean.

I – Remi Tictoc – Nutritionist can tell you how to get clean.

REMI *hands* **HARRIET** *a horrid looking green drink.*

If it looks like it came from the bottom of the bin, it looks great.

(Slide 18)

I have ordered for you this lasagne they make special for me here, in the vegan café, it is made from beans and grasses.

The meat is made of beans. The pasta is made of grasses. The cheese is made of beans and grasses.

This food is clean.

Thin doesn't exist. Fitness is an illusion. If the body is clean – it's working. You don't have problem. You don't get older. You don't have fat. You don't die.

If you are clean you are swift and cool. You smell neutral. Animals are drawn away from you. You move seamlessly from one season to the next. Summer. Autumn. Spring, Winter. Spring. Autumn, Summer, Winter, Summer. Done.

I have all kind of clients on my programme. Models. Swimmers. Nobel Prize Winners. People with really unusual bodies. Bits and pieces hanging off them. Here. Here. There. It's disgusting. But now all of them are really clean.

I've made a lot of Euros with my programme and I'm using my Euros to publish my next book. "Are you fucking boring? Stop."

So. Getting clean. I'll break it down. I'll do a full body scan. Because the thing about women is they aren't good at being whole. Which is of course because they are made almost entirely of sea water. Brine. So you have to slosh about with them, mentally, yeah?

So I say you need to be clean – here, here, here, there.

And I start with the hair. Why? Because if the eyes are the windows of the soul. The hair is the curtains. And men. Men like hair yeah? Because it reminds them of spaghetti. And that's good. Be-cause men like to eat. Even non Italians. So hair, keep it clean. If you are serious then wash it.

Face. I have my face ironed twice a month by a guy called Pepe in Kentish town. I lie down on the ironing board and he just fucking goes for it. It's hard to balance and I have to take Solpadeine for the painfulness. Because it hurts. It really fucking hurts. But my face looks nice and flat and it's clean.

Neck. The neck is the worst enemy of the woman. You can have your neck removed and I would advise it if you can afford. Just head – body no problem. The neck is flippy and its flappy, it serves no medical function at all. It's hard to keep clean because the flaps soak up filth particles. Disgusting. If you can't have your neck removed wear black polo necks – every French person knows this. An illusion.

The nails. To keep clean healthy nails – it's magnesium yeah? So that's milk. But you can't have milk as it makes you fat – so – you look at photos of cows.

REMI *shows us a photo of a cow.*

To clean the liver, it's good to clap your hands a lot while you drink your rosé, as it keeps it moving through. Singing like this is good for the spleen (*Sings weirdly*).

The rest we know. You wear shoes one and a half sizes too small to make you stand tall, you bal-ance your head on an invisible shelf, like this, your smile into your vagine and you never say sorry and rarely thank you.

You want to get to a state where if we had an Armageddon, nuclear holocaust, and we started eating human meat – like we maybe should – you would be hunted first because you are clean and desirable to eat. Birds of prey and prey. I think about that. I give that a lot of thought.

HARRIET I gave it a bit of thought. Then I went home for a cup of tea. I wonder if tea is clean. I just feel most relaxed when I'm just at home listening to Radio 4...

HARRIET *is in her London home.*

Desert Island Discs theme tune.

I like Desert Island Discs so much. It's so calm, and the music's so nice, so inspiring. Kirsty seems really lovely.

And last week, you know who was on? Who else is French? The detective Pascale Sucre! With the little grey cells. From the TV. And he is played by an actor who is my absolute hero.

He's DANIEL SACHET.

What a confident actor.

Kirsty asks him: "After going deep into character, how do you leave them behind at the end of the night and go home as yourself?"

Daniel says: "When you are in a theatre play. You have to say goodbye and go home as yourself."

Kirsty: "Literally say goodbye?"

Daniel: "Yes. I remember doing a production in London's West End. *Titus Andronicus.* I was playing (*pause*) Titus, which is a very, very difficult and complex role. He actually goes mad. And a dear friend of mine, a psychologist, came round to the dressing room after the show, glass of fizz, and he said – 'You can't do that, you can't do that Daniel, you can't do that every night.' And I said: 'What?' And he said: 'You can't do that every night and not get out of character, you'll drive yourself crazy.' I said – 'I am out of character – what are you talking about?' He said – 'You're not. You're not'. He said – 'What's your birthday? What's your agent's birthday? What's

Rosencrantz's birthday? Guildenstern's birthday?' (Those are Daniel Sachet's dachshund's names). 'What's your address? What's your telephone number? Come on, come on. What's your phone number? What's your phone number, man? What's your phone number?' And do you know? I couldn't remember any of it. And he said... 'There you are. You are not present. You are not out. You're still in. There you are.'

"And do you know Kirsty in that moment – it was true – I was not out, I was in, I was not Daniel Sachet, I was still Titus, I was not in London's glittering West End, I was in Rome, it was not 1987 it was... fucking ages ago, and I didn't have a phone number, I had – 'Hey Lucius, if you need me I shall be over there by that rock. '"

"My friend said – 'what's your phone number?' – 208 654 1654 I said. 'Again.' 2086541654. 'Again.' 208 654 1655 – (as **HARRIET**: It's hard to say it the same twice as I'm just making it up.) And I got out. I got back. But it took twenty-six or twenty-seven minutes, I'm better now, I'm faster, I can do it in twelve or thirteen, but I still have to do it every night, look in the mirror, glass of fizz, run the digits and return."

Kirsty is silent. Presumably in awe. Then she asks the question that any of us would... "But Daniel – how do you do the amazing voice of Pascale Sucre?"

And he says... "Well Kirsty, as an actor my body is my instrument so I naturally speak in a very low belly voice but Pascale Sucre is the world's most important brain – so I must travel my voice down here from my belly up to my lower chest, up to my upper chest into my throat and up to my head and the top of my head and then I start to add the accent (accent starts) of the most famous detective that Europe has ever known – with ze leetle grey cells."

Exit **HARRIET**

The year is 1533. **HARRIET**'*s ancestor enters carrying some feathers.*

Music: Greensleeves

TUDOR PHEASANT PLUCKER *(West Country)* Ello! I be a palace cook
for King Henry VIII. God bless his massive soul. The thing
about us Tudors, is we eats a lot of meats – from bob cats
covered in gold leaf to Henry's favourite… pheasant ice cream.

Peacocks are popular. It's easy to kill a peacock by strangling –
because they have long but tiny necks. You have to have a
sword to kill a swan as they're violent bastards but taste a tiny
bit sweet, like chicken but with icing sugar. A popular dish be
a Turducken – that's bird inside a bird inside a bird inside a
bird. For that you have to coerce a swan to eat a chicken who
has already eaten a small grouse who accidentally swallowed a
sparrow, you have to be quite lucky as the odds are against you
finding one, but strangely it does happen.

I hate to cook an ox. They are hard to strangle as you have to
hold their necks tight, which is hard as us Tudors have very
small hands. Slit the skin down the nose, then you have to peel
them. My son, Perkin, helps me pull the skin off into two long
pieces which we make into sleeves for a woman's gown. He
loves learning new things does my son, the three w's – wittling,
wattling and reading.

Pheasant is the staple this time of year. We have so many at the
palace that sometimes they push each other out of trees and
kill people madrigaling beneath.

I likes to fry 'em up with mushrooms and goldfish, I likes to
grate 'em into parsley mash, I likes to get the shire horses to

stamp on them and hide them down the well until they become ice creams, but I don't likes to pluck 'em. They get under the nails and they smell all woody.

So my husband Perkin plucks them. He's a fine pluck is Perkin. And my son "Perkin the second" too... I expect we'll have a long line of bird folk after us. But it's just as well it's Perkin who does the plucking. As one day last week Henry took terrible ill after eating a pheasant ice cream, heaven knows why with the care we take with the well, but he sends forty strong angry knights to ride down to our shit hole shouting: "Where be the pheasant plucker?" Luckily for him Perkin had got stuck in a priest hole that morning, and wasn't at home. "Give us the pheasant plucker", they hollered, "If you values your life". And just then little Perkin wanders out, picking his teeth with a feather...

I throws down the badger I was peeling, and I shuffles out of our hole.

"He's not the pheasant plucker!" I emoted. "He's the pheasant plucker's son, and he's only plucking pheasants till the pheasant plucking's done."

And before they had time to even ask...

"I'm not the pheasant plucker. I'm the pheasant plucker's wife and when I'm plucking pheasants it's a pheasant plucking life."

Audience are encouraged to sing reprise: "He's not the pheasant plucker he's the pheasant etc as above"

But on the whole I don't do it, see. And they laughed. They came in for a minced sparrow on crackers and all was well. It was close, mind.

HARRIET *makes more plans in her diary. (Slide 19)*

HARRIET Thanks great great great great great Granny for giving me some pluck. And Granny was right. Learning, that's key. That was on my list. I'll take myself to an open day…

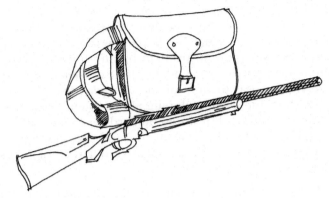

HARRIET *is at a university open day.* **IRENIE** *is giving a talk.*
(Slide 20)

Music: Alison Balsom Concerto in E-Flat

IRENIE   *(really posh)* Hi. Welcome to the graduate open day or
something. MAs and things like that. (MA is short for masters.
MA...sters?)

Investigative journalism. I'm doing an MA. I don't know what
it means really. But it's amazing. But I'm just sort of pissing
about. There's all these terribly clever boys on my course, but
I'm never completely sure what they're doing, just being so
sexy and amazing in lovely sexy sort of jumpers, investigating,
and using all these amazing words. And I just don't really know
what I'm doing. What am I doing?! There's too many journalists
anyway. There's nothing left to write about. Absolutely nothing.
I wanted to write about the glass ceiling but apparently it's
disappeared so I can't. Nothing.

And then with all the blogging and tweeting and tindering, well
you know. Hectic! Simple pleasures eh? I like it at home. I love
walking. And smoking. And riding. Every day when I'm here
I go with Mummy and it's just amazing. Out in the field with
the alpacas. Just so amazing. They're so hairy and gorgeous and
snuffly and furry. Sorry, could you understand what I just said?
Daddy always says it's so completely impossible to understand
me! I'm so sorry. He's just so depressed that I didn't turn out
more like Joanna Lumley.

Best thing about London – Proms. Alison Balsom is amazing isn't she? They say she's the best trumpet player in the world now. On her album the Torelli piece was written for "natural" trumpet – when the instrument had no holes or something, and it was made out of wood. Or stone or something. And that Czech piece was written for the *corno da caccia,* the hunting horn! Imagine us all galloping about listening to that? Jolly good fun. Although it would be hard for her actually to ride in that dress. I like her *so* much…and she's so slim. Such a tiny waist and lovely hair. It's amazing to have both. I mean the trumpet and the looks, isn't it?

Yuh. You could do an MA or something? And live in London. I live in London. In a flat and everything. But I go home whenever I can. It's so quiet and peaceful with the chickens and the pool table and everything. Up here it's so hectic! The parties, you know? At home, I have dinner every night with Mummy and Daddy and whoever is there. Not saying a word because what's the point if Daddy can't even understand me! He keeps suggesting things for me to write about like Syria and UKIP and Angelina Jolie type of things. And I'm like, look, it's all been done.

Have you seen the Tate? Seen the Vermeer? The light, and how it goes behind on the wall, and on the skin of her hand in a very soft way. He paints his scenes next to a window, so you can understand where the light is coming from. Everyone says the light is amazing! The light. Amazing. The light's amazing! And just that girl, she's so simple isn't she? So lovely. And all that blue. Calm.

I'll probably end up being an air hostess or something. Well I can't seem to play the trumpet or investigate much! Or maybe I'll just shoot myself. Get one of the hunting guns. Strip off completely naked apart from my riding boots and go into the gym by the tack room and stand on the Swiss Ball looking into the mirror and put the long cool gun into my mouth and shoot my amazing little brains out. They could daub my blood on their faces before they sit down for the soufflé course. They could scrub my guts up off the rowing machine. They could feed my organs, one by one, from a bucket, to the hounds. Amazing. Or some sexy little trolly dolly. Some slutty little air hostess. Hilarious. They'd love it, wouldn't they, the parentals. Amazing.

HARRIET I didn't really know what that posh bird was on about. This London thing isn't really working out...

HARRIET *and* **MUSICIAN** *sing* –

Suggested tune: Ironic by Alanis Morissette

WHAT WAS THE INFORMATION AND WHAT WAS THE COURSE?
SHE WAS HECTIC AND SHOUTY,
AND SHE LOOKED LIKE A HORSE.
AND IT'S SLIGHTLY FRUSTRATING,
DON'T YOU THINK?

MUSICIAN
IT'S SLIGHTLY FRUSTRATING,
I REALLY DO THINK.

BOTH
IT'S LIKE RAIN ON YOUR FALCON DISPLAY,
IT'S LIKE JESTER – WHEN HE FUCKS OFF AWAY.

HARRIET
BUT TOMORROW IS A BRAND NEW DAY.

MUSICIAN
BACK TO THE THERAPY OFFICE.

(Therapist's voice) "Come in Harriet, please take a seat."

HARRIET *opening the toy box.*

Box. Weird little animals...

Then I heard a voice...a voice of a dissident who knew the truth. It was Kanga...

HARRIET *takes a kangaroo toy from the box.*

(As Kanga, Aussie) G'day mate. I can't reveal my identity but – this is not the rural idyll it appears to be. There are three rabbit families and the white ones are supremacists. *(Slide 21: white rabbits hold swastikas)* Extremists. *(slide 22: rabbits holding swastikas)* Unspeakable acts take place. It's not the rural idyll you suspect. There are needles under the garden BBQ set *(slide 23: needles under the garden BBQ set)*, sex *(slide 24: toys having sex)*, sex *(slide 25: toys having sex)*, sex *(slide 26:*

toys having sex), drugs *(slide 27: toys taking drugs),* backstreet abortions in the pink nightlight nursery *(slide 28: this in the pink nightlight nursery).*

HARRIET *puts the kangaroo toy back, shocked.*

Maybe Mr Kanga has a fertile imagination, maybe I do…maybe my therapist just likes playing with toys and has got me to join in…

I was just legging it out of the therapy office when I ran into a handsome man/boy/male.

HARRIET *is outside the therapy office, runs into the* **BOY.**

MUSICIAN *plays* **BOY.**

"I think she's a nutjob" – I said.

"Yes – me too" he said.

I came to London to meet new people and I've spent all my money on playing with squirrels and talking to weirdos.

BOY – Well – how about if I take you out tonight? I know a lovely little traditional authentic French bistro. It's called… Café Rouge.

Great.

BOY – Eight-thirty – it's a date.

HARRIET *is in a romantic restaurant. (Slide 29)*

Sound of clinking glasses.

HARRIET Hi waitress, may I have the most enormous glass of your cheapest wine please? I'm waiting for a date. I'm waiting for the therapy room guy. I guess that's where you meet people in London. I'm great at dates. No problem. The thing about dates is you just have to be good at asking questions.

I'm dating. I'm out there. Well, I'm in here. I'm online. I have a profile. I have photos, in one I'm wearing a hat. There's one with a paella in shot. To show I'm, well, you know, I've been around. Not like that. I have a few facts about myself on there. That was hard. Really hard. So I wrote "Owns a lurcher", "likes macaroons", "up for some laughs". You know KIL. Keep it light. It says that I grew up in Kent. The truth. That I prefer short men. I do, underdogs. But my main thing – the thing I really have to offer – I can't write down on the form. I can't explain it unless you meet me. What do you think it could be?

Could it be – I'm great at...asking questions?

That's what people want really. What men want. Quite simply to answer. Makes you feel you can really do something. You can answer. Very good for the confidence, answering. How did you get into Deputy Finance Managing then? What's your favourite season? You must feel happy your sister finally found love in Barbados? Wow – so much salt? Do you like birds? Do you watch a lot of porn? Do you think Labour's looking ok? Did you know the ideal PH for your vagina is somewhere between a grapefruit and rain? That's true.

But the only problem is, by date three I've asked a lot of the questions in the world. How heavy would a micropig be? Is a macro pig just a pig? Thoughts on *Birdman? Thunderbirds? To Kill A Mockingbird, Bigbird?* Too much?

And I just think – maybe one day. I'll meet one. An asker. Who asks me a question. I mean – is that too much to ask? Does it matter? Would I even answer?

Are you out there? Do you speak English? Hello? Is it me you're looking for?

Date arrives.

"Oh Hello? I'm Harriet. Yes it's me you're looking for…"

Suggested music: Hello by Lionel Richie.

HARRIET *downs her wine, beams at audience.*

HARRIET *is on the train home. (Slide 30)*

Train sound.

From offstage **TRAIN TANNOY.**

HARRIET *(offstage) has got hold of the train tannoy.*

HARRIET *sings.*
TALL AND THIN AND YOUNG AND UGLY,
THE GIRL FROM IPANEMA GOES WALKING.
AND WHEN SHE'S WALKING EACH ONE SHE'S WALKIN GOES... YIP!
TALL AND SLENDER SHE'S LIKE A SALAD.
THAT SWINGS SO WIDE AND SWAYS SO GENTLY THAT AS SHE'S
WALKING THE DOG SHE'S WALKING IS HO!

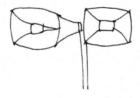

(spoken over tannoy)

You're the 11.23 to Norwich, the 11.23 to Norwich.

YOU ARE THE 11.23 from SAINT WATERLOO home to
Norwich – and I have the tannoy – olé.

Shit I've dropped my nuggets.

Yes. I have the tannoy. Ladies and gentlemen congratulations
felicitations and good night. It's me Harriet on the mic. On the
mic – er-a-phone. Get your danger on.

(sings)

I'M BLUE LADA DE LADA DA – LA DADA DEE DADA.

God it's dark out the window.

So. How was your night folks? How was it? Did you have a pizza?

I did not.

I did go on a date to the Red Cafe. And onwards to the bar called – Buzz Bar? Fizz bar? Was it? The Eagle's Nest? The Horse and Heron? You know. In a way. I'm not totally sure what the bar was called, but I loved it guys. I loved it.

He was a pleasant enough fucker. But I wasn't that bothered. I just wanted to get home...to Jester.

Did you know owls actually can't turn their heads all the way round? They would unscrew and fall off. Jester! Is there a falcon onboard?

Never drink anything green. Eugh. That's what my dad says. Never drink anything green. Or anything blue. Never drink out of a test tube. Never trust a man in a white van.

Sorry.

To any white vans on the train. I'm sorry – I didn't mean to be rude. This is for you.

(sings)

RHYTHM IS A DANCER,
IT'S A SOURCE OF CANCER,
YOU CAN FEEL IT EVERYWHERE,
2, 3, 9 WASH YOUR HANDS AND VOICES,
GET THE TRAIN AND JOIN US,
EVEN IF YOU JUST DON'T CARE. YIP!

(spoken)

Had enough of that one Shhhhhh.
Someone's coming!
Someone's coming!
Someone's coming!
Oh no that's a fire extinguisher, that was there before.
Just nice to have a drink and a talk and a proper talk you know and I'm just going to be sick I think... I think...? No.
Oh, still more chips in here.

So – (*interview style of Graham Norton*), an epic night was it?

– Yes.

– Tell us about your dreams, tell us about your dreams…

– Well Graham…

Graham Norton isn't sounding very Irish is he? Try again.

– (*Terrible Irish accent*) Tell us, what of your dreams?

Well Graham – I dream of being a good whole person in a peaceful time, I dream of a garden with a trampoline and children – and lettuce and a bird feeder yet also – a career of shoulder pads and clipboards – also – pirate dreams of swords and sailing and some very cross bones, a parrot who's a bit of an arsehole, an island, those massive red crabs, never having to move straw around or throw steaks.

– I like you.

– I like you Graham. You make a lot of cock jokes though. Too many. I think.

– Thanks love, for the feedback.

– That's ok. God. I'm tired.

I've got bbq sauce on my tights.

(*sings*)
HERE THERE WHEREVER YOU ARE, I CAN KNOW THAT YOUR HEART WILL GO ON

I hate that, I hate that one. Everyone on earth hates that song.

HARRIET *has seen a guard.*

Hello.
Your uniform is sexy. You look cross.
Your uniform is sexy. Cross.
Oh, I'm not supposed to be doing this… I'm in trouble.

The tannoy is clonked down.

Train sound.

HARRIET *returns to her field. (Slide 31)*

Music: same soaring anthemic American prairie type music as start.

HARRIET It's so good to be back in my field...Yip. Yip.

(Shouts up to the sky) Hey Jester, where do birds invest their money? On the stork exchange.

Oh Jester, I want to tell you about all the weird people I met. But wherever you go, there you are.

Jester. Jester. *(Spots him up in the sky – gasps)* Jester!

Exit **HARRIET**.

Enter **JESTER** *(a falcon, cockney, feathered, smoking)*

JESTER So, I'm Jester. Falcon.

I fucked off for a bit. To eat bats.

I thought it might do her some good to be honest.

She thinks she's so hard to work out – but I know everything about her. She's too big for a falcon. And she still hasn't learnt to fly. She's not hairy enough to be a wolf. Quite. And a bit slow. She's not a porpoise or a tortoise or a beaver. She's not a stoat or a goat. She sings these naff Ibiza classics and gives it all of that. But I don't understand a word. I'm a bird. But she gets in such a flap.

HARRIET & JESTER *dance together (suggested music: King by Years and Years). In the dance* **HARRIET** *beckons for* **JESTER** *to fly down to her, he refuses. She implores him. He refuses again. She implores him again. He shrugs – Ok.* **JESTER** *returns to* **HARRIET**. *(If one actor is playing both – blackouts can be used to switch between characters)*

HARRIET & JESTER *are together.*

MUSICIAN Harriet and Jester, what a team.

The **MUSICIAN** *sings the song King by Years and Years,* **HARRIET** *joins in, a soulful duet.*

MUSICIAN And there in the field they found each other again, and the world turned, and things carried on, and somewhere in West London, a yoga teacher is walking into a studio and asking her students to take a deep breath in through the nose...

Enter **YOGA TEACHER**

Music: yoga chanting. (Slide 32)

YOGA TEACHER ...in through the nose and out – not through the nose or mouth but through... the perineum. Closing class by coming up into moutain pose. On your feet. Normal standing up pose. And calling to mind what you already have because a bird in your hand is worth two in your bush. Elevating the left hand and journeying it towards the right. Bringing the hands together. Like a car crash, like a pigeon into a window, like the beautiful union of a man and a woman. Or a man and a man, or two transgendered men, maybe one who has had the work done and another who is just in the process of talking it through with counsellors and friends, or a swan and a swan or cat and a dog or two foxes, no – because that sounds horrendous. Why? Because foxes have barbed penises. I mean, it's complicated enough for us but at least no-one has a barbed penis. At least, not in my own personal experience. Yet. Left hand journeys towards right, it's clapping isn't it. It's just clapping.

The End

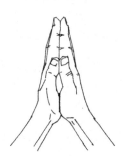

List of slides

A projector shows slides/pictures throughout

Slide 1: an empty sky

Slide 2: list of birds

Slide 3: yoga candle

Slide 4: therapy chair

Slide 5: a toy farmyard animal woman

Slide 6: a toy house

Slide 7: three toy farmyard animals

Slide 8: male toy farmyard animal

Slide 9: many toy animals

Slide 10: exotic animals e.g. kangaroo and koala

Slide 11: a toy holiday camper

Slide 12: a toy owl

Slide 13: a toy frog

Slide 14: back to owl. Owl wears a little orange gilet and no pants

Slide 15: a toy farmyard animal family

Slide 16: penis balloons

Slide 17: vegan café

Slide 18: lasagne

Slide 19: Harriet's diary from the field. Second page. Another list

Slide 20: open day

Slide 21: funny slide of white rabbits doing these things

Slide 22: extremists – rabbits holding swastikas

Slide 23: needles under the garden BBQ set

Slide 24: toys having sex

Slide 25: toys having sex

Slide 26: toys having sex

Slide 27: toys taking drugs

Slide 28: backstreet abortions in the pink nightlight nursery

Slide 29: of date restaurant table

Slide 30: train

Slide 31: big sky

Slide 32: candle

Property list

As indicated in the performance notes the staging of the play is up to each designer/performers' ideas and inspiration. I performed the piece alone (apart from Luke Courtier, as Musician at the Bush Theatre). My set had grass, leaves, a feathered chair and a Silver Birch Tree (made by talented designer Simon Wells). Also, a projector with slides (see list of slides).

Many of my costumes and props had feathers on them, to tie them together thematically in an avian way.

Props/costumes

Musician's Guitar

Harriet:

Yellow wellies

Yellow waterproof jacket

Dark green suede falconer's gauntlet

80s sunglasses

Sturdy bag

Steak

Rat (fake) on a string

Diary and pen

Yoga Teacher:

Feathered head band

Feather dream catcher necklace

Yoga mat

Therapist:

Box of toy animals

Palm Reader:

Feather Boa

Cock balloon

Remi Tictoc:

Saffron silk turban

Green drink

Photo of a cow

A radio

A cup of tea

Tudor Pheasant Plucker:

Apron and mob cap

A few pheasant feathers

Irenie:

Boots

Blazer

Alice band

Clipboard

Glass of red wine for the date

Jester:

Feathered gilet

Beak

Fag

Lightning Source UK Ltd.
Milton Keynes UK
UKOW05f2112181116
288007UK00001B/35/P